Aqua Curves

Aqua Curves

Karen Braucher

Selected as winner of
the National Federation of State Poetry Societies
Stevens Poetry Manuscript Competition
by Peter Meinke

NFSPS Press

This publication is the 2005 winner of the National Federation of State Poetry Societies Stevens Poetry Manuscript Competition, an annual competition with a deadline of October 15th. Complete rules and information on the purchase of past publications may be obtained by visiting www.nfsps.com or by contacting:

Doris Stengel, NFSPS
Stevens Poetry Manuscript Chairman
1510 S. 7th Street
Brainerd, MN 56401

Book and cover design by Tommy Herrmann

NFSPS Press Book Editor: Margo LaGattuta

NFSPS Press
3128 Walton Boulevard, Suite186
Rochester Hills, MI 48309

This book was set in Adobe Jenson Pro.

ISBN 0-9767006-0-3

for Roger, my Neptune

and in memory of
Richard Hugo,
my first poetry teacher—
so deep, so kind

Show me the way to the ocean!
                    —Rumi

Table of Contents

Outside the Hall of Mirrors

She sees reflections—
stretched like pulled taffy,

her head deformed upward,
a hydrocephalic, or, body

squashed, a squat gourd,
a face like a telephone and

little flipper arms. The next
makes her lascivious, a porn star,

nubile and twenty years younger.
She walks faster. A glimpse of

talons, her face with fangs.
Eyes closed, she gropes for

the door—

outside the Hall of Mirrors,
she is relieved to be in light rain.

A tiny crowd has thrown down
their carnival tickets in mud,

stomping and laughing. They are
yelling, "Long live language!" in

a hundred different tongues.

Cassiopeia from the Hot Tub

Her body sometimes
melts, like the divine—

solid turned to liquid
transformed to vapor—

the back strained
from carrying

her Andromeda
becomes heaven:

constellations shimmering
through steam, shifting

slightly each night
as the planet turns,

and just then the laws of
physics may amuse anyone—

a toddler, a scientist,
a mother submerged in stars.

Wanting Less

Eleven empty easels sit in a room without
abstract paintings or collages. Let's be
this large empty room painted white
with a shellacked wooden floor. A room
of silence, naked and wanton. A life
with more hiatus. That moment of
vacuum, timeless. Let's be
rivers that run through the middle of houses.
Upwards light buoys us
to surge through cities of clouds, a place
never dreamed, realms of noble terror
and delight where we become brushstrokes.

Jellyfish

To carry such 3D squiggles
half-baked or crazed
notions   streaming
calligraphy   time-lapse
neon streaks

To expand   a parachute
sink slowly
to the ocean floor   rise
upward   opening
and closing
my crazy umbrella   my filmy
mushroom cap

To swirl   galaxies
in deep space
seen through a telescope
a love that keeps spiraling

To pulse slowly my odd
frills   my oneiric membranes

suspended

like smoke   without bones
translucent   inside a glow

To ascend   dust
off the desert
seemingly innocent
a feminine
rocket
lavishly shedding larvae

To sting
explode on contact
this *medusa*　with
breathtaking poison
paralyzes
your intricately obvious
way of seeing

Recovered Memory

At the time I was reclining
on Dr. Freud's couch, a vision
of loveliness, and I realized
I was not telling him
a dream, but of my former
life among coral reefs, caverns.
I could again see flocks
of gaily colored fish flying
through turquoise waters.
"It was real!" I cried out,
shaking the plush sofa.
The hem of my apron
was dripping wet.
"Let us not get agitated,
Fräulein. You remember your
hysteria last week, my dear,"
said the solemn doctor, sucking
on his pipe, furiously writing.
"Yes, Herr Doctor," I whispered,
but inside I was not meek.
I was a sea nymph again,
mating with a mortal man,
and thus acquiring my soul.

Beatnik Baby: Kinetics, 1962

There is a vitality, a life force, an energy
that is translated through you. There is only
one of you in all of time.   —Martha Graham

She sailed cafés, jazz clubs,
          bohemian Harvard Square.
Brilliant & willowy,
          my eldest sister
                    launched "happenings"
in our living room:

Three sisters—black
          leotards & cut-off tights—
                    tiptoed, pliéd,
                              leaped & spun, barefoot,
          while our brother beat
                    bongos like a fever.

Our rapt audience,
Father—habitual suit—
Mother—dress, girdle & nylons, heels—
looked on, smiling,
from stiff ladder-back chairs.

With one lamp as spotlight,
          our black-and-white TV
                    shrouded, Roberta
                              spoke. Her voice floated,
                    charcoal smoke,
          while I opened,
                    closed to each twist.

I was eight. She was the living end.

So I swirled, shuddered,
     danced the deck of her skiff,
         dove rhythms, my first
syncopations, rode
       the wake of her mystery
           with electric feet,
       gained my own centrifugal force—
a sea-beast frolicks,
     back arched or concave,
a woman rises in spirals, long hair
       whipping in the mist.

To Leave with No Suitcase

like my sister did. To leave
without words, breathless.

To look at the desk, forsythia. To go
as bombs start falling.

To know you're leaving all your
belongings. What good is goodbye?

To go, go, just the clothes, your back,
wallet, passport. To disappear

toward Paris, bridges over the Seine.
Perhaps not Paris, perhaps Fiji?

To leave like spinning a globe
as a child—closed eyes, finger

placed lightly. To embrace
fear like a long-lost friend.

Palace

Deep cobalt
where you float,
smooth.

Voices below,
silly, superficial
oompahpahs.

Where are you?

Occasional
saxophone, flute
ululation.

All the little deaths
resonate
inside a cello.

Lying in a
sky-hammock, staring
at stars, you feel pity.

How else to feel
for those who've never
been here? You withdrew

from everyone, you lulu—
that's how
you held on.

Helen Keller Enters the Ocean

My whole body alive, touched
by sink and swell, I was
quivering joy, rocking. Rush of

water over my head, waves tossed,
toyed with me, back and forth,
loss of footing, turned upside

down, hands and chin slammed
rough sand, which way up? I was
sudden terror. Nothing but my prayer:

Not yet. Not yet. Then the ocean again lifted
me up and threw me down on the shore.
Clasped in Anne's arms, shivering,

still rocking, panic subsided, my mind
filled with questions
and my hands spelled into her hands,

"Who put salt in the water?"
But I have known icy fingertips
more chilling than the ocean,

and fingers that radiate the sun.
I am blessed by pleasure—
swimming, rowing, tandem bicycling,

reading first in English, and then
French, German, Greek and Latin:
O goddess of fortune,

with power to raise our perishable bodies
        from low degree or turn
the pomp of triumph into funeral…

And I have been intimate with trees,
climbing, swinging, caressing
their bark, smelling their

flowers. Perfume, textures,
words fill me. Every day I
plunge in.

Baudelaire's Siren

She's naked except for
her jewels, of course.
Two goblets reflect candles,
her brown skin, brocade
draped from their bed,
her naked undulations. Later,
Charles draws away from her.
He's a hard, salty cracker after
tastes of sweet chutney. He thinks
she's more luscious than trees
trembling in rain, most cruel of
women in her seduction. This is
before long letters are exchanged
articulating their hatred, their love—
acrid, sweet as hashish, stultifying
as opium. Jeanne knows it's time
to pack her carpetbag, disappear
into Paris. She covers his eyes
from behind, pressing against him.
"You're going to remember me always,"
 she whispers. She's about to tell him
the truth, when he groans, wraps his arms
round her, rolls her again on the bed.
In his head: *Her arms and legs, her reins
and her thighs' spices...* She will leave often,
threaten never to return. He'll lament
her nature, his used-up money. But
being lost can lead to such celebration!
Squeaky springs make them laugh, moan,
while bedposts murmur, "Give up, give up!"

Ragamuffin Coats

Ragtag scraps sewn together, she's showing me,
says, "You can work here and in just a few hours
a day you can make lotsa money!"
It's an old ramshackle bungalow she's
rummaging through.

Outside
donkeys and dogs in the sunny dirt,
I put my best foot forward
in this rat-trap interview, trying to get the best damn
job possible, till she says, "Oh, we *all*
make the coats here. After you get the knack, you'll
do it in a jiffy."

Strangely beautiful, each coat different,
like something from the Andes
or Kathmandu—
but looking like they're put together
by bag ladies who inexplicably achieved focus.
How they're put together, these ragamuffin
coats don't try to hide. Unpretentious.

Like Joseph, could I
have a razzle dazzle coat? Not
from my father, but something
made by my own hands and eyes?
Despite everything, I'll save
odds and ends, make
things ragged,
with colors shining.

Bouillabaisse

We know there's no recipe.
Some omit potatoes, others scallops.
Some favor certain kinds of fish.
Others insist on prawns in the shell,
or prefer them naked.
As cats caress our legs
like hedonistic demons,
we invent our own fish stew:
red snapper, seabass, sole,
leeks and lemon rind
dropped in steaming water.
Here are some rules. There must be
tomato purée, garlic, cayenne pepper.
You can skip a splash of wine
but it tastes richer, better. Simmering as
we dance across wide kitchen planks
in our old blue jeans, I add
parsley for you, I add leeks,
potatoes, olive oil, and onions.
Shrimp are in, mussels in their shells.
Still there's something essential,
something to turn our stirring,
make this stew rise. Look for
the purple crocus, upper tip
of the pistil of the flower,
where pollen is received,
only in certain fields.

Fable of the Mermaid and the Robots
after Pablo Neruda

All these robots were in the lab
when she entered completely naked.
Recently emerged from the sea, she
understood nothing. The robots hummed,
came close, took many measurements.
The brain scan, body scan, and telemetry
flowed over her luminous flesh. She was
not afraid nor ashamed and simply sang
her haunting song that had no words.
One robot addressed her, "You are not
logical. My programming leads me to
the conclusion you can not exist." Another
robot said, "My memory shows only one picture
that looks like you, and it's from a children's
book. Who are you?" A third spoke then
in its monotone, "Can you help the humans
who created us? They seem to have lost
all purpose." The mermaid's eyes were
opalescent and unfathomable. She laughed
a little wearily and left by the alley door.
Hardly had she entered the ocean than she
flicked her double tail and disappeared.
But the robots kept churning through their
memories and logic loops, wore out
their CPUs trying to understand.

Dark Horse

Fear doesn't stop at a fence.
It grows larger than the prairie sky
when we take the step we do not want to take
because the heart says must.
You were a long shot always,
the horse no one would gamble on,
would steer clear of, most likely.
Now, sitting on the fence, my cowboy boots
thick with dust, I clench and unclench my hands,
and wonder how bad things can get
before black thunderheads drench us both
in prayed-for rain.
Fear grows stronger than this old corral,
but not stronger than my hands.

Doppelgänger

I have lived as a careful wife
though my husband knows of
my one scarlet secret:
I might go back to sea,
wanderlust long ago sewn into
my indecent fish scales,
stitched with emeralds, lapus lazuli.

I am unable to let him go—
his passion, so earthly, fills me.
With jewels, waving sea grass hair,
I'm his rowdy German *meerfrau,*
bewitching like white sea foam,
my abalone mirror and harp,
gathering dust.

He might come home weighed
down with drudgery, open
a heavy door to formica
and linoleum, or instead
barnacled treasure chests,
seaweed cascading out of windows,
marine music, whale and dulcimer.

Is it arousing for a fisherman,
my uncontrollable mutability?
My *gestalt* inexpressible
at village bratwurst barbecues,
but real enough past midnight
when he starts, bolt upright,
gasping for air, his legs tangled
in damp spiraling sheets,
his dreams full of shipwrecks.

Wasps

Not only the threat of the sting.
Your bodies, bulbous, hovering,
obscene, I loathe, and your
angry buzz, like lawyers arguing.

Perhaps you're excited
with your creation,
nest stuck in the eaves,
an insect Mesa Verde.

Who can say humans are
dissimilar, with our
constant traffic whizzing
round skyscrapers?
Looking up at your home,

alive with crawling bodies,
I think barrios of Ecuador.
Brothels of Calcutta.
Stock exchanges.
Parliament. Or perhaps

you are monks,
droning a spiritual
syllable, loving your world.
Everywhere beings
sing their self-importance.

Her Mother's Obsession

Hundreds.
Little and large. Glass, stone,
porcelain. Jeweled, painted
or rough hewn. Frogs
everywhere her eyes alight
in her mother's home.

Frogs that
can not jump or swim or croak—
was it some misplaced, shortchanged
dream of moving between worlds,
her daughter wonders. *But someone*
so afraid of death...Or were they
her emblem for a world where
a kissed frog is still a frog?

At first,
they had seemed benign,
whimsical. After decades
of sinister proliferation,
hunched, knobby beasts
with bulbous eyes sit silently.
A pile-up of tiny multi-colored
tree frogs, poisonous frogs,
leapfrogging frogs, big silly frogs
with tennis rackets, some
lounging like people on lily pads,
with and without crowns. Sad
spawn. No enchantments.

Learning to Play Violin at 45

Her father's soft ghost has begun to play
a Bach minuet with confidence, grace.
His battered violin now fills her days

with formal practice, festive matinées
of acting lofty, no alcohol trace.
Her father's soft ghost has begun to play

arpeggios of roses, fluid clay,
messy fingerpaints, lavish paper lace.
His battered violin's lifting her haze.

Her stiff *pater* pushed his music away
with drudging and liquor, a frenzied pace.
Her father's soft ghost has begun to play

mellifluous songs for swinging soirées
she hosts to crack his rigid carapace,
blasts the Marseillaise in white negligée!

Though she never heard or saw him play,
she can imagine his enraptured face.
Her father's soft ghost, she's begun to play.
His battered violin now fills her days.

Le Cri de Mélusine
after a French folk tale

If you had only listened, Raymond,
and not bowed to convention,
impatient husband with no imagination,
now most cursed in *tout le monde.*

Six days a week I was the perfect wife and mother.
Couldn't you respect my one wild day?
My bath where I flipped my fish tail (*outré!*)
was sacred, till you peeked, gaped at The Other.

Over our village I fly, a wingèd serpent,
circling three times, sobbing a woman's grief.
I will leave forever. Our family life was brief.
Children, I'll always care but I won't repent.

Paint on Paper

Exhausted by both hemispheres
of her brain, she accepted that she was
a hackneyed expression.
She wanted to think
large thoughts and make herself
no particular person.
She wanted to go nowhere.

No longer sad, nor happy,
she suspected this was what
maturity felt like. She wanted
to erase herself, finally,
from all her paintings,
the paintings of blue women dancing,
and make no particular person.
She wanted no symbols anywhere.

She came to *ikebana*, flowers
arranged in an asymmetrical sweep,
the fire of crimson leaves
against white speckled, raked gravel.
Staring at flowers carefully arranged,
she thinks all existence shares

the fate of paint on paper moved
by a human hand, shares the fate of
a person used terribly. Most beautiful
when half-ugly and almost something
else. Scratched up, scarred, rippled,
mottled, tinged with wet fading leaves.

The World in Miniature
—Japanese Garden, Portland, Oregon

Place of stillness, why have I
waited so long to return?
White flowers grace a cherry tree
that was stark last time I climbed the hill.

Water pours down the bamboo spout,
into the small stone basin,
where a sparrow sips.
I have lost all my worries.

I come upon a gardener pruning
along the narrow path.
"Let me get out of your way," he says.
"You are the way," I reply. We both smile.

Almost lost in Japan, "the way" is
kept alive in out-of-the-way places.
When you bow to the aromatic tea
in the earthen bowl, you bow to the universe.

It is calming to view the world in miniature,
as if one were up in the clouds.
This pond edge could be a whole harbor,
the mushroom lantern its lighthouse.

On an ancient lantern, covered with moss,
figures in lotus position are almost worn away.
This is what we must become to reach
the sacred mountain.

I sit down to view the garden of sand
and stone. No symbols. Only shape.
The ripples in raked gravel
remind me of nothing.

Becoming Ambidextrous

She walked through air as if it were water,
brushed teeth like it was new, serious business.

Her heart hurt all the time, or was it the other
place behind her heart? Her mind, ragged,

let her left hand move first, pressing keys,
picking up paper, though her right had

always been so sure, precise. Someone
she didn't know was becoming her. She was

alone. She was going deeper. Sunsets were
roses on fire. Letters exploded in mailboxes.

For the first time she was operating
on raw nerve, but carefully. Every move

counted. She was staying one step
ahead of the void, so far, both hands now

sketching jagged lines and arcs, exploring
innumerable surfaces. She consulted with

strangers, shredded rose petals, scribbled
phrases on the backs of envelopes,

rubbed charcoal into parchment. When
she met people, she not only stared into

their eyes, she looked slightly away from them.
She knew they were cobbled constellations,

best viewed from many angles.

Iphigenia, Coming On Fast

It was my very last Lucy in the Sky routine.
Grass grew thirty feet high. I was a worm.
(Father had phoned that he must *please the gods*.)
Only my death could change the wind? I cowered,
waiting for a monster-movie-sized bird
to peck me dead. Everything came down
to blood. I asked a tiny floating college boy,
"What's this stuff do to your brain anyway?"

I felt staccato—why should I be sacrificed
so troops could sail for Troy? I began to crawl
across the field to my dorm room where
students sat bored with birth control pills,
Dostoevsky. My white dress fluttered
as I looked into unloving Father's face—
a field of dead grass. Did he even have
a decent *theory*? It was time for me to travel,
geographically. A thousand ships could wait.

Moving West

For the first time not treed in, her eyes trace
the horizon line, clear in all directions.

Exultant, she remembers the Bostonians'
raised eyebrows when they heard

she was moving to Colorado. Could it be
they were afraid to stand under such

a large sky they were nothing to? Nothing to
the Ponderosa pine, nothing to the tall men in

cowboy boots sauntering down Larimer Street,
eating antelope or elk at the Buckhorn Exchange,

nothing to the hang glider catching the updraft
near the Boulder Flatirons in dazzling sun.

She breathed the brisk air that comes from
moving to edges, up above tree line,

on cliffs where the heart beats fast, taking in
the circumference of sky. Impossible
to return home. Impossible to return.

Finding Gray
in memory of poet and teacher Richard Hugo

Gray reminds me of you, Dick, and college days.
You hated Colorado, the constant sun, the way
ski resort people breezed. I've found my gray land,
Oregon, as you had Montana in your large hands.
In class we started with black/white, soft/hard, water/rock.
Does the mind try to find gray like confused fish? Knocked
away from moorings by birth, do we start to drown?
The crazy kids are the ones who write it down.

Poverty danced with you for so long. I was entranced
with good words in your class but afraid. Sexton's dance
with death was that year. Looking back is always an illusion.
But you were real as a truck driver from Duluth. A fusion
of grit and wave. So big in spirit, you shocked the room
when your voice rolled, and you were kind. The boom
of your sadness broke over us, deeply American, gray
with the betrayal of the Indians, gray with the broken ways

of workers of the plains. You were humble, soft-spoken.
I didn't cry till years after your death. With older men,
writers, drunks or worse, I said how much I'd missed.
They understood. I remember how you fished,
how a wife turned to the wall while her husband wept,
how lunatics were kissed by your sorrow. Rhythms leapt
like rip of tide, the moon always going wrong.
You kept the lid on, but just barely, and not for long,

master of one-syllable words, of all that drowns.
The crazy kids are the ones who write it down.

Breathing Under Water

Shimmering like the insides
of abalone shells,
blues, greens & silver, she
weaves her body through seaweed.
How else to dive down
to find what is hidden?
Over her head, a creamy swirl of pearl,
she seems to carry the moon,

but maybe it's a circle,
a mirror, a shipwrecked relic.
Her hair floats in tangles
round her body, jade-like plants
and rivers of bubbles spiral
close to the unbelievable
tail, whale-like, iridescent.

When her tail is gone, at kitchen
sink she stands washing dishes,
singing to the birch trees. She holds up
each circle like a pearl in the window
to see if it shines. She cannot stay
too long on earth telling stories to
strangers and stones, wild grass
and feral cats, fish in tanks
and foam. She has learned
to breathe under water,

she has done several things today
already that she knows to be
impossible. She has turned
into a squirrel, a frog, a rat,
a baby. She has turned
into a secret about how
men drown, even on land.

Cajun Shrimp Bacchanal

1. The Shrimp
      2 doz. large shrimp

We're going to mainline you,
no salad on the side,
no rice on the side,
just you, crescents of pink flesh,
plump half moons,
just you, dressed up and ready
to be taken to bed, to be devoured,
to be enjoyed completely.
Ocean ambrosia, we are impressed
by your jumbo size and flesh.

2. The Seasonings
      ground red pepper
      ground black pepper
      salt
      crushed red pepper
      thyme
      rosemary
      oregano

You have that flair, that *je ne sais quoi.*
How do you make it look so professional?
A man at the stove turns me
feminine, effusive. It occurs to me:
Men must be *made* to stand at stoves!
It's the biological imperative!
All this hot stuff excites—my feet
dance on the tiles, my arms wrap round
your flannel waist, my fingers run
down down down your denimed legs.

3. The Sauce
    1 stick plus 5 TB unsalted butter
    1 1/2 tspn. minced garlic
    1 tspn. Worcestershire sauce
    1/2 cup shrimp stock
    1/4 cup beer at room temperature

An expert male is unbelievably sexual.
An expert female is often one who
doesn't look like an expert. These facts
of life are hard to take, except
when your man is a gourmet chef.
All is forgiven, just give me those
juicy, buttery, spicy shrimp.
Drop them one by one down my throat
between long cool sips of bottled beer.
Ah, a chef, to have a chef, to love the chef!

4. How to Do It
    Combine seasonings in small bowl. Combine 1 stick butter, garlic,
    Worcestershire, seasonings. Mix in large skillet over high heat.
    When butter is melted, add shrimp. Cook two minutes, shaking
    pan. Add 5 tablespoons butter and stock. Cook and shake pan two
    minutes. Add beer. Cook and shake one minute.

This is Louisiana food, bold, adventurous.
Makes your head sweat, your heart pound.
Zydeco music—crazy accordion, singers
raging—accompanies our feasting.
Your jeans are so soft, I run my wet
hands down them. Ah, a chef,
to have a chef, to love the chef!
Finishing your shrimp, you perform
the benediction: "Cajun food is
such succulent poison."

Saudi Arabian Letters

1.

Dear Katrinka, old lover,

In the market, everything:
spices, brass, daggers,
cell phones, jewelry.

I held up my hand
to show your height.
It wasn't difficult

to fit you—Arabic women
from northern Africa
are tall, slim.

But blonde is ugly here.
The shop owner brought
the *adebye*,

long-sleeved, black robe
to the floor, and
the *scarve*,

black covering
for your head and face.
Only eyes and eyebrows

show. Beauty for
a woman in public: eyes
and a scent.

The fabric is light,
synthetic. The brand,
"My Fair Lady."

Bargaining started at 300 Riyals,
collapsed to 100 because
you weren't coming

from America for
hem alteration. All
women—teenagers,

housewives,
even Lufthansa stewardesses—
wear these in 110 degree heat.

Why do you want
this costume?

Why do you wish
to blend with the night?

Love, Richard

2.

Dear Richard,

Remember
you're married now.
I hold up the robe.

One could think
of it as slavery.
But there is power

in invisibility.
I want to wrap
myself in darkness

and be judged
only by my eyes
and my words.

I add this cloak
to my closet of disguises,
my repertoire of tricks

and humiliations.
Thank you
for sending it.

They say the veiled
wear gorgeous
underwear, fabulous

shoes, and I will
do my best.
Look for me

and you cannot find me.
Smell the wind, see
eyes on fire—

I might be there.
What is love
but a veil?

Caviar

Who/what is an aphrodisiac
on the brink of extinction?

Salty black beads, we're
helpless before your/our

compression. A species
that devours other

species, tails
in our mouths,

we desire
(vodka coup d'etat!)

the sour of
revolutions.

We desire
origins—the entire

ocean, a womb—
heaped on our cracked heads.

Earrings

In spring, his wife found a curve,
a question mark, on the car floor.
She put it in a plastic bag, pinned it
to the kitchen bulletin board. The two children
watched. The next day, he returned it,
still in the bag, to his lover, telling her
that he'd convinced his wife it was nothing.
But the lover knew that the wife knew
because she was a woman.

That summer, she lost an iridescent one
when they were alone at his family cabin.
Half-dressed, on their hands and knees,
they searched the floor and bedclothes
for abalone shell outlined in silver.
She felt elated, spent, but he turned
methodical, insistent, his urgency
so harsh it made her think he was
fearful of legal evidence.

By autumn, he demanded that her ears
be stripped before lovemaking,
an intelligent idea but to her ruthless,
as if he were trying to strip her away
and leave only passion. That night she took
the fiery golden filigree from her ears
as she straddled him on the bed,
as if discretion could erase
the dreams which woke their spouses.

The last time, he came to her home
through snow drifts, picked up earrings
one by one, like small prayer objects,
with a look of great yearning.
Then he asked if the really exotic ones
he'd never seen—bronze ovals
from the far east, tiny flower buds
along the rim and fragile dangles
hanging down like rain—were

what she wore when making love to
her husband. He desired to picture her
in detail, but she froze, her lips closed.
He saw that she wanted to keep
things separate, as though that
would somehow keep everyone
disentangled. He noticed her ears
were bare, and then she touched
each earlobe, her hands trembling.

Ancient Catch & Release
after a Chinese folk tale

A woman who swings from clouds,
swims as a fish, who can make
a man be in two places
at the same time—
wouldn't any man
desire her desperately?
Chen the nobleman first spies
her swinging from the sky
after he's shipwrecked.
Her hair a raven cloud,
her robes exquisite silken
landscapes. Her swing flies
back and forth, the ropes
going infinitely upward
as he gapes. Dragged
before her by guards,
he expects to die,

but *she* bows to *him*,
for he once threw her back
in the sea, a flashing fish
caught by the emperor.
She's Princess of Tung Lake,
Shape-shifter, Sorceress,
Queen of Misty Realms.
When she swims, she becomes
a fish, but Chen saw something
in the eyes of that fish
that made him
plead for release.

Lovers they become,
languorous, god-like,
and she, the Perfect Lover,
makes certain he's also
at home even while they
intertwine. A friend leaves
Chen feasting with her on a barge
but the same afternoon, finds him
back in his village,
a family man, drinking with pals.
When Chen dies, he smiles.
His coffin is remarkably light.
The men open it. Inside?
A curl of seaweed, drizzle of water.

How To Stay Married

The perfect marriage is, they say,
a blind woman married to a deaf man.
Or is it a deaf woman married to
a blind man? Failing to achieve
these physical variations,
it is helpful to think
of marriage as ocean waves—
swelling, breaking, sucking, forever
pounding and returning.

With what authority do I speak?
My dossier lists Katrinka von Brioche,
25 years with the same man! Not one year
all voluptuous or all gritty.
Doesn't marriage flow? In and around
two people? Observe tranquil ripples,
later choppy whitecaps, also gale force
winds with tempestuous seas,
detritus from yachts, pollution
from toxic dumps.

Learn to float, practice subterfuges,
expect repetition. All step-by-step
guide books are an insult. You must be
lucky or slow-witted. You must
want a shared history of beds,
a trousseau of disguises, a growing
knowledge of diplomatic strategies.
You must buy ear plugs or
opera glasses or funny hats.

After a while, you must be
a boat, or parts of a boat—
yesterday the rusty scupper,
today gunwales, tomorrow ballast
and bailing buckets. You must
be a motor, a sail, a paddle.
It's helpful to enjoy the view.
It's helpful not to think
about the lack of life preservers.

The Floating Brothel

Below, the Mulatto piano player begins a riff so cool
     and syncopated that men roll and groan on deck.
Female laughter cascades and ricochets amid the tinkling
     of wine goblets and cutlery
While black hands caress white keys.

Above, men cast and cast again, searching for fish
     to fight with on this rolling tropical highway.
They want tuna, not the slashing strikes of wahoo,
And leaning forward in their white linen suits,
     they shout prayers to the gods of the sea.

Intricate, intertwined ribbons of life give rise to this
     flesh and fish,
A road rushing warm and fast, leading only to Newport and death.
But all aboard praise dark meat steaks: blackfin tuna grilled.
Sighs of wonder and lust give way to smacking lips.
It doesn't get better than this: the animated suspension gift.

Captain adjusts his fishing harness as a tuna fights his line,
Diving to the bottom strong and wild. Hook to reel-in
Can be a long time. The moon touches his tan face,
Intent on a catch, and the scream of the drag fills the night air.
He feels the wind smack and thinks of her below deck.

Curled up with hookah and book, Celeste exhales a stream of smoke.
It rises in the cabin air and hangs there.
Feathers, furs, and jewels float by as she rolls in silk.
She's getting there. By day she was in harness,
Gripped the heavy rod, and brought in fighting fish.
Now, night has crawled in.
Pulling back white cotton skirts from legs sinewy and brown,
She arches her back and tells the world to enter.
Now, before the jazz piece ends.

The fighter on his line has stopped his crazy dives.
He feels a winner coming on.
Whispering and swearing, he coaxes it in:
A shiny thirty pounder destined for the pan.
He breathes in salt, breaks into a smile.
Off port can be heard the shore-based sounds
Of steel drums, soka, and skootch.
He unties his harness and heads below. She needs him now.

Intricate, intertwined ribbons of life give rise to this
        flesh and fish,
A road rushing warm and fast, leading only to Newport and death.
Now all aboard praise dark meat steaks: blackfin tuna grilled.
Sighs of wonder and lust give way to smacking lips.
It doesn't get better than this: the animated suspension gift.

Mrs. Fitzgerald Discovers Her Red Hat

after an Irish folk tale about a merrow (mermaid)
and her cohullen druith (magic hat)

Finally I'm alone. Children all grown,
and Mister Fitzgerald traveled to town.
I'll sweep crannies with my feather duster
though housework bores—I'd rather eat oysters.
Sometimes I glimpse a strange, sad woman
in the glass. There should be something red and ribbon.
Sometimes I arrange bluebonnets with yarrow
though my spirit longs for kelp, like a merrow.
Odd dreams, frothy, floating…Lord, what a web
on the fireplace chimney. What's this? A snub
of fishing net's fallen down from a cubbyhole,
and crumpled red cloth with ribbon rolls…
I remember this hat—*cohullen druith*. Embroidered,
sewn with feathers, ribbons with pearl borders
to tie under my chin. How I used to hunt
for this, my mother's gift to me. In front
of the dressing mirror, I'll try it on. Green.
My hair's green! I'm thin, sleek again,
all from this hat my husband hid from me.
All this time, I've been longing for the sea,
where fish flash, hide in grottos, my brothers
and sisters swim and dance. I'm smothered
by you, Fitzgerald, you weak two-legger!
My time has come—you can be a beggar.
What's time but a trap I accepted? What's love
but a net holding me fast? Give me my trove
of treasure. Years peel away. I'm salty and sweet.
All my girlhood loves down in the deep still beat

for *me*, want *me*, dance for *me*. The diving,
dolphin riding, swirling and conniving,
all the motion I've lost in this wooden box!
Like death they are, humans, like boatless docks.
The doors have blown open and sea songs call
my scales, soon my tail, and diaphanous shawl.
Red hat, crimson joy, enchanting and small—
down to the sea with me, to the emerald hall.

To Her Surprise, What the Postmodern Tarot Deck Predicted

To come all this way and find that you are
at the beginning. Your task is to hold fast.
Do not take more journeys.
Go home & stay home. Stay quiet & work
with your hands. Read and think and make small,
quiet, careful things. You must not depart.

Everyone and everything will be
transformed. Without TVs, without hollow men, without
wallets. Cook leek soup over a slow flame. Sew clothes
with a silver needle. Curl around your partner,
murmur of rain, pine needles. Murmur of deer
in the yard, nibbling new flowers.

Mixing Turquoise at Nehalem Hardware Store in Summer

We stare at paint chips in shades of blue
to change our white cottage door near the dunes—

from Crystal Palace, the palest hue,
our eyes move downward to

Robin's Egg, still too white, to Spring Breeze,
slightly brighter, more zip, to Caribbean, the eyes

begin to rest here, swim in warm saltiness,
then lower to Tropical Sea. Here winds tease

the sails of ships through phosphorescence,
the Lost Boys are coming, all independence,

to play with mermaids in the cove
while Captain Hook is away, till we move

our eyes down to Peacock. It says, "Look at me!"
No, too showy. We go back to Tropical Sea,

point to that shade, and tell the man
that one, please. He adds blue to a can

of white, then almost as much green,
a little black. The can is jiggled by machine.

At the cash register we ask to see our shade
before we pay. A muscular maid

who is well acquainted with mixing paint
pries off the lid, and yes, there skid

Tinker Bell, the Lost Boys shooting down
Wendy from the sky at Tink's command,

and Peter himself emerging from the rousing
waves, mermaid scales still stuck to his trousers.

Brief

Lately, when I look at people's faces, they peel off.
I see secrets, corpses dangling in moonlight.

I'm afraid of what I know and how alone we are.
Not like battalions of bats inhaling mosquitoes over

summer swamps. To want to live forever sounds
foolish at mid-life. Have you seen how petals

dry and wrinkle, brilliant colors fading to off-white?
One day you'll wake up and look in the mirror.

Your face will be limp, gray mold. Know
you can survive more terrible things. Choose

to look out at the world with different eyes. Try
being a small ceramic mermaid in a goldfish

aquarium, in a box inside other boxes,
algae growing on your face, the fish flicking

their tails round you. Are you surprised?
Pleased by your obscurity? You can go

out into the world, glad life was given
to you, even if it will be taken away.

Odysseus Raves, Lashed to the Mast

This is the time of sunstroke & no shadow. I alone
　　　　hear a hum, a rustling silver. No wind & our sails down,
　　　　　　only oars dip. My men don't look to shore.

They hope to pass this isle alive. Hum turns to unearthly
　　　　voices. Shimmer-girls, erase my Penelope's face!
　　　　　　Like falcon-,　　like dolphin-girls,

you cavort, dive & sing. Untie me, men! Obey your captain, your king!
　　　　Everything we were told must be false. They change bodies,
　　　　　　woman & animal, at will, & sing of harmony, nothing else.

∞

I alone glide and tumble on this song. Hover, tendrils of hair,
　　　　ravishing breasts, soft fawn-colored wings. My body rises,
　　　　　　strains.　　　　Why survive　　all our travails

only to row like slaves, no hope for the glorious
　　　　spontaneous act?　　　Don't bind me tighter.
　　　　　　Fiends.　　　Better I'd left you swine, forever

with Circe. Humdrum sailors—beeswax in your ears—
　　　　you're rowing　　*away*　　from paradise!
　　　　　　　　　　Deaf eunuchs!

∞

Exquisite silences and sound. Greater than Circe's bed.
　　　　All I've lost, found. Arch, beckon, vibrate
　　　　　　my spine, Soul. Ambrosia, let's devour

each other's coast. I bleed, twist for you, heavenly host.
        Enlighten & lighten, Light. Bite through these ropes.
            When to listen, when not to listen? I see no skulls,

ships' hulls, only succulent lips, tongues. Death would be
        so small. Insatiable. Glistening. Take me.
            Lick   me   clean.

∞

I alone glow gold. Am erect, ready. I want
        nothing but you, you, and you—wingèd and finned
            bodies elect. Pluck me like a string.

I'm a slave to my rules. Should I have stoppered my ears?
        All knowledge, past & future, all art could be
            mine, you sing, if only I follow your shower

of promises. I've damned myself. I only planned
        to listen—to be the only one to listen & live to tell.
            I couldn't imagine   ecstasy so close to hell.

Autumn in the New Century

was coming with stiletto high heels,
"total ownership" of an A-line skirt
in shades of jalapeño and mustard,
comfortable classics. Cheese was
all the rage, and heads of unusual
lettuce, tattoos too, the A.C.L.U., and fashions
celebrating tribalism. Everyone wanted
a shorter commute.

        Instead, autumn came
in shades of ash, soot, disfigured,
falling head over heels, the entrepreneurial
economy in suspended animation. It came
with slashed payrolls, empty
airports. It came with wailing and silence.
No one would invest in a kite factory.

Autumn came wrenched with twisted
buildings, body parts, thoughts
of gas masks, flat-heeled boots
for evacuation, pantsuits
for crawling under, knee-jerk anger
and caution. It came with eyes
squeezed or streaming, wearing
videos of thousands of funerals,
donating blood to the Red Cross.

Autumn was a new dislocation
holding orphans and many flags.

Crème Brûlée at the Mermaid Café

Do you like burnt sugar, custard so smooth?
Chocolate crusts cupped in salty fingers?
Come to the café. Here, everyone's dreams
are sunken treasure ships. On a barstool,
the owner, Typhoon Windlass, sits.
Crusty lusciousness. Wavy russet hair,
turquoise work shirt, toes long and tanned.
Her hair streaming down in waterfalls,
Typhoon may tell a story about her boat.
Halfway between hyena and foghorn, her laugh
rolls in waves from her throat across the bar.
Now her eyes search clamshells, calamari plates.
When she looks at you, your heart beats faster.
Your heart is a pirate, sailing before the wind.
Down the windswept beach at low tide, dusk,
Typhoon walks barefoot, slowly comes to a halt.

A creature moves, not wholly of this world,
wild as a shark, green eyes dart and alight
on abalone, sea anemones. Water stretches
to the horizon, turns different colors with each
change in light, like a mermaid's song
at dusk on a forlorn beach. If you are lucky,
you've met Typhoon Windlass and spent
some time drinking her jade tea beneath
spider plants, staring out to sea from
her rocking chair draped in seal hide.
No one knows where she goes, when she'll
return, but some hold their breath as they enter
the café, hoping the waterfall hair, glowing eyes
will flash with news from a different realm,
a place where our clothes and names are removed,
and we swim awestruck in glittering foam.

Medusa in the Checkout Line

No milk in the fridge
       so here I am,
              pantyhose bunched
      in my dainties.
Hellish day, hemorrhoids,
       and the boss demanded
             umpteen spreadsheets.
      I focus on breathing,
like my shrink always says,
       but still I feel my hair
             lift and sway, spiral, writhe.
      I get jazzed
on the tongues, little red flickers
       in the periphery,
             then the glorious hiss—
      I could go to the front
of the slime! Everyone's
       turned to stone,
             and the cashier
      with averted TV eyes
faints dead away.
       I grab my milk and float
             through the door. Another
                serpentine holiday.

Her Daughter's Collection

Against the side of the beach house,
a row of dried branches and driftwood leans—

one is huge and forked like a giant compass;
she uses it to draw large circles in the dirt.

Another is short and sharp like an old quill pen;
she crouches and carves words with it in wet sand.

Other sticks are for fencing with friends.
Still others are wands that turn you to stone,

to monster, to pterodactyl. Most adults
see just a row of useless old sticks.

One is long like a beast of burden's yoke;
she carries it across her shoulders

with pails at both ends, down to
her excavation projects near the sea.

She's Back

She wore a necklace of doorbells,
a nightgown of Calypso music,
and had already woven her golden hair
back into his bedclothes. His ears,
she whispered, still smelled like
fresh violets after ten years. As he
touched her, extraordinary curlicues
arched across the wallpaper of the attic
and strings of antique buttons,
flashing shell and stone, swayed
from wall hooks where the purring cats
touched them, curious, with their paws.

The world opened for him
like rose-colored mums
in a cool spray of rain.
He basked in sofa comfort,
beer warmth, jewelry dazzle,
childhood bathtub rosiness.
From the kitchen, wafting up
the stairs came the aroma
of simmering soup heavy with garlic
and new promises.

She had come back, with her
crazy paper birds, her kitchen waltzes,
and her slender but brazen hands
touching his face, fresh basil and tarragon
still clinging to her palms. He felt
the shock of her monkey laughter
and knew she'd unpacked
her calico bag of autumn leaves,
eagle feathers, and amulets.

In her eyes he saw a Sunday morning
of coffee cake and fresh cut flowers,
The New York Times spread
across a tawny sunlit carpet,
the cats sprawled in fish breakfast
contentment, and she curled beside him,
nuzzling his arm, while nonchalantly
stealing the Travel Section.

Instructions

Among hands, be the cat's cradle,
among keepsakes, the one-of-a-kind,
among footsteps, the syncopated soft shoe,
among scissors, the one that scallops.

Among questions, be the unanswerable,
between twins, the sixth sense,
among pairs, the lost glove,
among colors, the autumn rose.

Among weapons, be a disarming strategy,
among doors, the one that opens to thin air,
among the shadows you find on the floor,
be the one that flutters.

Curves

That was the summer I fell asleep in German
  and woke up in French. I lay down on the earth,
    stared up through a three-dimensional labyrinth
      of dark branches stretching toward sky.
        Curves are so much more caressing than
          straight lines, *n'est-ce pas?* Who has time
            to look at parabolas? Could I express only
              a parade of diversionary questions? *Nein, nein,*
                the German inside demanded, *Gib mir Antworten!*
                  I went to a party and tried only to ask questions
                    and answer none. I was a spy, intimidating
                      to at least two persons. Questions are curves,
                        without closure. Could one spend a whole evening
                          on a stroll through someone else's mind? How
                            refreshing to encounter unfamiliar corridors.
                          No one is throwing up skeet and asking me
                        to shoot. The parade massed and snapped
                      to attention, goose-stepped away. Replaced by
                    tendrils, drifting pine needles. When I awoke, I was
                  la belle étrangère, omnipotent in my voluptuous
                listening. I could coax even the waves to speak.

Notes

I am moved to say that some of these poems are not autobiographical.

"Helen Keller Enters the Ocean": This poem is based on an episode from Helen Keller's life as described in her autobiography, *Story of My Life*. The passage in italics about the goddess of fortune is from Horace's Odes.

"Baudelaire's Siren": The brief passage in italics is from the poem "The Jewels" by Charles Baudelaire. His lover was Jeanne Duval.

"Bouillabaisse": This French fish stew is not complete without saffron, which comes from crocus flowers. This poem was inspired by Old English riddles.

"Doppelgänger": *Meerfrau* is the word for "mermaid" in German.

"Curves": The German translates, "No, no, give me answers!" The French translates, "Is it not so?" and "the beautiful stranger."

Acknowledgments

These poems or earlier versions of them were published or are forthcoming in the following publications: "Wanting Less" in *atelier*, "Recovered Memory" in *The Chaffin Journal*, "Earrings" in *Diner*, "Ragamuffin Coats" in *Fireweed*, "Jellyfish" in *Friends of William Stafford Newsletter*, "Paint on Paper" in *The Issue*, "Bouillabaisse," "Breathing Under Water," "Helen Keller Enters the Ocean," "How to Stay Married," "Mixing Turquoise at Nehalem Hardware Store in Summer," "My Daughter's Collection," "She's Back," "To Leave with No Suitcase," and "Instructions" in *Manzanita Quarterly*, "Cajun Shrimp Bacchanal" in *Nervy Girl*, "Le Cri de Melusine," "Mrs. Fitzgerald Discovers Her Red Hat," and "Odysseus Raves, Lashed to the Mast" in *the new renaissance*, "Dark Horse" in *The Oregonian*, "Doppelgänger" in *The Oregon Review*, "To Her Surprise, What the Postmodern Tarot Deck Predicted" in *The Paterson Literary Review*, "Wasps" in *Pool*, "Finding Gray" and "Moving West" in *Poetry and Prose Annual*, "Learning to Play Violin at 45" and "Saudi Arabian Letters" in *Rain*, "Curves" in *Rattle*, "Becoming Ambidextrous," "Cassiopeia from the Hot Tub," "The Floating Brothel," and "Crème Brûlée at the Mermaid Café" in *The Worcester Review*.

"Wanting Less" appeared as a poster on Portland's buses and trains as part of the Poetry Society of America's Poetry in Motion program in 2003. "The Floating Brothel" was published in *The Worcester Review* as the first place winner of the Worcester County Poetry Prize, selected by poet Stephen Dobyns. "Dark Horse" won a prize from the New England Poetry Society. "Finding Gray" was honored by Portland PEN Women.

Many thanks to Literary Arts, Inc. for providing two Literary Fellowships. A residency at Caldera in Sisters, Oregon, allowed me to work on this collection.

Thanks and Cajun shrimp to Peg Miller and Garry Gitzen for the Mermaid Festival in Wheeler, Oregon, where I read poems surrounded by paintings of mermaids and ships. Crème brûlée to the poets in the Pearls and the Portlandia Collaborative who helped inspire or critique poems.

Special thanks to poets David Biespiel, Patricia Bollin, Robert and Julie Brown, Helen Marie Casey, Angie Chuang, Maggie Chula, Raphael Dagold, Christine Delea, Ron Drummond, Leanne Grabel, Jennifer Grotz, Sarah Lantz, Rodger Martin, Judy Montgomery, Carolyn Moore, Susan Firghil Park, Paulann Petersen, Donna Prinzmetal, Eve Rifkah, Cassandra Sagan, Willa Schneberg, Penelope Schott, John Surowiecki, Judith Taylor, Pat Vivian, and Laura Weeks for their kindness over the years.

Some of these poems appeared in a chapbook entitled *Mermaid Café* (Pudding House Publications, 2004). I would like to thank publisher Jennifer Bosveld and her staff for their work on behalf of many poets.

Without the love of my husband, Roger Tobin, and my daughter, Betty Li Tobin, none of these poems would have gone out into the world. I promise to take you both to Sushi Boat forever and always!

Margo LaGattuta and Tommy Herrmann, you're the best. The mermaids sing for you.

About the Author

Karen Braucher is the author of *Aqua Curves*, winner of the 2005 Stevens Manuscript Competition (selected by Peter Meinke), and *Sending Messages Over Inconceivable Distances*, finalist for the Oregon Book Award (selected by Maxine Kumin), as well as two chapbooks, *Mermaid Café* and *Heaven's Net*. Her poems have appeared or are forthcoming in *atelier, Diner, Fireweed, hipfish, Manzanita Quarterly, Pool, Puerto del Sol, Nervy Girl, the new renaissance, Nimrod International Journal of Prose & Poetry, The Oregonian, Oregon Review, Paterson Literary Review, Rain, Rattle, The Spoon River Poetry Review, The Worcester Review*, and other places, including Portland's buses and trains through the national Poetry in Motion program.

Braucher has won the Grolier Poetry Prize, the Worcester Poetry Prize, the Bacchae Press chapbook competition, and two Oregon Literary Arts fellowships. She has had multiple careers in education and business and has three graduate degrees, including an MBA from UNC-Chapel Hill and an MFA in writing from Vermont College/The Union Institute. She studied English literature, graduating Phi Beta Kappa, at the University of Colorado at Boulder, where she took a senior seminar with late poet Richard Hugo. While writing, occasionally teaching, raising a child, and running a small poetry press known as Portlandia, she lives and swims in Portland, Oregon. She is originally from Massachusetts.